THE TWELVE SPIRITUAL
LAWS OF THE UNIVERSE

THE TWELVE

SPIRITUAL LAWS

OF THE

UNIVERSE

A Pathway To Ascension

Santi

Nothing in the world is single,
All things by a law divine
In one spirit meet and mingle.

— Percy Bysshe Shelley,
Love's Philosophy [1819], st. I

CreateSpace Books
7290 B. Investment Dr.
Charleston, SC 29418

FIRST EDITION

ISBN - 13: 978-1453828557
ISBN - 10: 1453828559

CreateSpace BOOKS is a trademark of Amazon, Inc.

To Laura

I am blessed to have my best friend, partner and spiritual guide by my side. Her wisdom and love sustain me in all that I do. This book is dedicated to her.

INTRODUCTION

All of us have had an awakening of our spirit by someone who came into our lives at a time when we were ready
for change. *When the student is ready, the teacher appears.* So it was with me.

I had heard of Elwood Babbitt for a number of years and
wanted to have a reading with him, but he was living on
the East Coast and I lived on the West Coast. At that time
in 1987, I was involved with a wonderful group of people
who wanted to establish a Metaphysical Center in Colora-
do. One of our group had purchased land outside of Colo-
rado Springs where we intended to set up our Center. We
invited Elwood Babbitt to come and share his gift with us.

He came and gave us a group reading which was very
humorous and light in nature. Mark Twain came through
Elwood and shared his slightly off-color humor, which was
wonderful. The following day, I was able to get my first
reading with Elwood. This reading changed my life. Dr.
Frederick Fisher came through Elwood and told me of some
of my many past lives, who I was in Spirit and why I had
elected to come to the Earth-Plain at this time. I was over-
whelmed by this information. It was like a fog lifted and I
could see who I really was. At this time I did not know Elwood very well, but I wanted to support him and his wonderful gift. In promoting him and bringing others to him for
readings, we became friends. The more I learned about

this remarkable man the more I appreciated him. Over the years and through other readings by him, I gained an even better appreciation of his gift to us. At one point in our talks, he introduced me to a couple of his books that he thought would help me in my quest for helping others. They were 'The God Within' and 'Talks With Christ and his teachers.'

After absorbing these books, I told Elwood that I wanted to teach classes on the immutable Laws of the Universe which had come from Vishnu. He encouraged me to do so and so I began to teach. As I'm sure you know, we teach what we need to learn, and so it was with me. These experiences have led to the creation of this book. I hope you find it beneficial.

Santi

A NOTE ON VISHNU

In Hinduism, Vishnu is one-third of the trinity of gods (Trimurti) who were considered aspects of one universal God, much as the Christian Trinity is considered to be three Persons in One (God the Father, the Son and the Holy Ghost or Spirit). In Hinduism, there is Brahma the Creator, Vishnu the Preserver and Siva the Destroyer, all aspects of the One. Vishnu is thus viewed as the lord who sustains the Universe and upholds its Laws. He was also called the Soul of the Universe and the Compassionate and as such was identified with the ideas of Eternity and Love. According to Hindu mythology, Vishnu has incarnated nine times on earth to save humanity from self-destruction (good vs. evil). Vishnu is also the arbitrator of all disagreements between humans or even gods. By interceding, he upholds justice and moral order with all. He is patient and has a gentle, merciful nature.

When Elwood Babbitt started to channel the *Vishnu Force*, the power of the vibrations was so great that he almost died. It wasn't until he finally recovered and was released from the hospital that he insisted Spirit bring in more Vibrational Engineers to facilitate a safer channeling of Vishnu. According to Dr. Fisher, those involved in spirit (Spirit Vibrational Engineers) did not know the extent of protection that was needed in order for the Vishnu Force to come through Elwood Babbitt safely. This extreme channeling had never been done before. Yet, Dr. Fisher (who was Elwood Babbitt's Spirit control) took full responsibility for the mishap. Fortunately for us and Elwood, this increase in Vibrational Engineers allowed the Vishnu Force to communicate to us through him without any subsequent danger to his physical body.

I had been privileged to have experienced the Vishnu Force come through Elwood once in Santa Barbara, California. I can only describe the experience as being very Holy and Sacred. Fortunately, I recorded the words of Vishnu and yet to this day it is difficult for me to hear his words over the Love of his vibrations. Not that the words are not clear, for they are. It is just that the power of Vishnu is so great that it puts me in an altered vibrational state and I feel the communication rather than hear it.

I'm mentioning this about Vishnu because I feel it is important for each of us to understand that what came from this Hindu God is priceless to anyone who wishes to become enlightened and free of pain. None of us need be a Hindu in order to benefit from this gift. Vishnu could care less whether we believe in Hinduism or not. All he cares about is bringing peace to humanity. On a personal note: I don't claim any religion exclusively. I believe that there is validity to all religions that embrace love over fear. Yet, it was my personal experiences with the Vishnu Force, through Elwood, that changed my life.

Below is a quote from Vishnu that came through Elwood Babbitt.

"I come to you from the universal ocean of vitality, from the Gateway of Eternity in this, the universal vibration, that hovers within all the galaxies and constellations, not in the dimension of space but in the vibrational spectrum that ascends from this, your earth condition, to the very apex, the tiny thread of creativity. It is my purpose to serve you in these moments when all vibrational influences are in direct alignment with what we are trying to achieve: the understanding of the brotherhood of man; of the full meaning of your existence and that of all men, and the full understanding of the principles governing all interrelated lives that will bring the reactions of every individual to the highest possible point of perfection."*

So what is presented here is my guided interpretation, definition and understanding of the Laws of the Universe as given to us by Vishnu. With each presentation of the Laws, I have included exercises that will help you understand their relevance.

---

* The God Within" by Elwood Babbitt and Charles Hapgood, pp 25-6

TABLE OF CONTENTS

TABLE OF CONTENTS (Continued)

GIVING OURSELVES DIRECTIONS
"THE WHY"

You see things; and you say, "Why?"
But I dream things that never were; and I say,
"Why not?"
- George Bernard Shaw, Back to Methuselah, pt. I, act I

To a greater or lesser extent, all of us question who we are, why we exist and why there is so much suffering in the world. These questions come from our pain as well as our inquisitive nature. Not only do we want to know how things work, but why things even exist. If we can learn to understand the laws that govern everything, then we have a greater opportunity to understand what is going on in the universe and our lives. Therefore, we owe it to ourselves to become familiar with and conscious of these laws as much as possible. Simplistic by design, they become intricate when we begin to examine them in detail. I believe that all the pain that each of us has experienced is because we were out of integrity with one or more of these laws. So the key to bringing peace into our lives is to study and implement a unity with these laws. All of us, by our very nature, need to resolve our many questions of "why?" Our inquisitive nature can be our liberator.

These twelve laws represent much wisdom passed on to us from not only Vishnu but many other Master Forces and Teachers in Spirit. They are gifts of liberation.

THE LAW OF ORDER

"Order is Heaven's first law." - Alexander Pope

Our challenge is understanding that everything in the Universe is guided by order, which is the methodical arrangement of things. What appears to be disorder or chaos is illusion. The more we explore the vastness and the minute, the more we confirm this truth.

When we begin to trust our intuition, we begin to gain a greater clarity of how the universe works. No matter how pragmatic or emotional we are, once we begin to sense the validity of the greater wisdom of our intuition, we know everything must exist in order or it would not be. Order is both physical and psychical.

This law is the lattice work of the universe. Its structure and pattern demand regular and harmonious arrangement. In the lattice work of the universe is the expression of the cycles of time. Sequence of events (time) can be defined as order. The organization of DNA is Order in action.

Order is the logical connected relationship of everything. Understanding that everything is interconnected and interdependent allows us to see this logical relationship.

It seems that it is humanity who chooses to go against nature. We alone try to mould nature to our desire and against its own natural direction. Case in point: global warming, pollution, etc. that are caused by mankind's concept that we are above nature. We must learn to respect

3

nature or we will become extinct. The Law of Order will weed us out of the picture. We must learn to flow with nature and not continue to try to mould her to our egotistical misconception that we are more important than anything else.

We must recognize that the disorder we feel in our lives is illusion. That is to say, that we create illusion by accepting fear as truth. When we begin to recognize that our disorder with nature, (the nature of self), is based upon a concept that we lack the value, support or love that others have, we are living with illusion. We create our reality. Everything that comes to us in disorder is created by us. So if our lives represent disorder, it is the circumstance of fear that our habits have created. All of us are creatures of habit. Habits come to us with childhood experiences. So if we are in turmoil, perhaps our childhood experiences gave us an unreal concept of truth. If we lacked love and/ or understanding as a child, our experience of this lack can create the illusion that we do not deserve love or understanding. We maintain the concept that we are alone and unloved. Yet this goes against the Law of Order and so we create sickness or pain out of disorder. So our challenge is to reverse this internal conversation so that we can begin to see the bigger picture of our value and that we have always been entitled to love and understanding. Every person needs love, respect, security, nurturing and peace. It is our natural need. Everything that we need is found in the universe. Our challenge is to recognize this truth and then simply accept the gift of reality. In doing so, we create the order we were designed to have and the peace that has always been our birthright.

Still, if we think we are more 'right' than people of other cultures, we create disorder. We may be convinced that our political system is better than others, but we would be wrong if we thought that we were better or more important as a people than others. This is the illusion created by our collective ego. Nations can be in disorder just as easily as individuals. So collectively we need to change the disorder in which we live in our nation so that there is opportunity for global peace. This could start, (as it has), with a movement toward being responsible for the health of the planet. Yet, the health of the planet can only come to fruition when there is health in each of us. I am not talking about perfection but rather tranquility with the Law of Order. Perfection is possible in the twelfth law, the Law of Illumination, but only if we live in the consciousness of all the laws.

A good example of a person with a disordered life is a young man I knew in the Navy. He worked as a clothes cleaner and since the ship we were on was a small one, he was the only one doing this job. I was also naive and very young at the time. So I did not recognize his anger and hate but assumed that he could be my friend. We would go on the beach together (leave from our ship) and hit the bars. I remember him saying; "Why don't we hit the beach and beat up queers?" I thought he was joking, but he wasn't. As I grew to know him, I realized that he could only relate to people through hate and anger, including myself as his so-called friend. To this day, I have no idea what happened to him. I believe he was headed in the direction of either being killed, thrown in prison or both. My guess is that he was terribly abused as a child and did not know of any other way to relate to people other than violence. Very sad and such a waste.

What we need to recognize is that all of us have a little bit of my Navy friend's disability of hatred and anger locked up inside which comes to the surface now and again. I remember Dr. Hal Stone telling me that he did not trust anyone who claimed they were on a Spiritual path if they had not looked at their dark side.*

---

* Dr.s Hal and Sidra Stone are co-founders of "Voice Dialogue," a psychological process of discovering the different personalities within ourselves. If you are interested in this powerful process of self discovery, contact:
Voice Dialogue International
PO Box 604, Albion, CA 95410.
Phone: (707) 937-2424,
Fax: (707) 937-4119.
www.voicedialogue.org
Email: info@voicedialogue.org
Ask for the name and phone number of a facilitator in your area. They also publish an international directory.

All of us have a dark side. There is a little bit of Hitler in all of us and until we look and acknowledge his presence we are living in a false relationship with ourselves and others.

So, I invite you to explore your dark side and see where you are in disorder with your soul and the universe. Then when you experience hatred or anger you will know where it comes from and why. The deeper you go into your exploration, the greater the opportunity for peace.

When someone cuts you off in traffic, what is your reaction and why? When you end up in an argument with your spouse, children or friends, what is the foundation for your anger?

Wherever there is disorder there is opportunity to resolve this conflict if you are willing to be honest and truthful to yourself. The Law of Order demands that there be peace within you as well as around you.

Exercise #1:

Since anger creates disorder, let us look at anger as our guide.

1. Take a small note pad with you as you start the day. Whenever you experience anger, stop and make an abbreviated note in your note pad so you can remember the situ-

ation. Do this throughout your day, then at the end of the day look at what you have written. Remembering the anger, can you tap into what caused your anger?

2. Now allow yourself to go into meditation and be with these questions one at a time:

What does this episode remind me of?

Did someone In my pasl make me angry in a similar ox perience?

If you discover that you are still angry with this person from your past, then I would invite you to write this person a letter. Use every cuss word you can think of. Express your anger and your sense of outrage and pain at what this person did to you. Then you burn the letter. The reasons that you burn the letter are two-fold. One, this letter is not about confrontation, it is about you. Two, when you burn the letter, you are allowing this energy to go into the higher realms, where at some point your abuser will have to deal with their karmic indebtedness.**

** There may be more to it than this. Your "abuser" may have agreed to interact with you in this way prior to the two of you coming into the Earth-Plane to help you move beyond this condition of anger. More often than not, there are more reasons for a situation than we are aware of.

When we are comfortable in expressing our anger to the ones responsible for our pain, we begin to heal. It is not about making someone wrong and you right, it is about honoring your pain and anger. When you gain an understanding of what caused your anger, you begin to put yourself in harmony with the Law of Order.

The larger truth is that this person is not responsible for your pain. You have a built in reaction to the situation that caused your pain. When you explore the cause of your pain, in this depth, you can better understand that it wasn't the person who caused the pain but a reaction within you. From this realization you can better understand that this person was/is your teacher.

Exercise #2:

Think of a rock, a cow pie (excrement) and a flower. Now challenge yourself to see where the connection is with all three of these and where and how they express the Law of Order. You will need to write down your observations and conclusions in a note book. (Your writing crystallizes your thoughts and conclusions more profoundly than just thinking about them.)

The reason for this exercise is to bring to you an expanded consciousness of the Law of Order. When you challenge yourself to see order in differing objects or life forms you gain a deeper understanding of where you fit into the scheme of things.

The next step is for you to pick three different objects from nature and then to challenge yourself to see the connection and how this expresses the Law of Order.

Exercise #3:

This exercise involves visualization and meditation.

1. Before meditation, make a list of all the things in your life that represent Order which gave you a beneficial direction, such as the order of your positive thoughts that directed you toward an expanded education.

2. Then make a second list of all the things that represent Disorder that took you in the "wrong" direction, such as fear of being your own boss in your own business.

3. Next, go into a meditative state and center your attention on your breath. Now as you inhale visualize bringing one of the listed Orders into you through your breath.

4. Then exhale one of the corresponding Disorders out of you. Concentrate on the bringing in this Order and casting out the Disorder with each breath. Do this as long as

you wish.

Note: Obviously, the longer you visualize this positive Order coming into you and the negative Disorder leaving you, the better. In choosing your 'Orders' and 'Disorders', please keep in mind that there is no duality, so 'Disorders' are really illusions.

5. Repeat this breath meditation exercise daily using a different order-disorder combination until you have completed your lists.

I will invite you to do a similar exercise with each of the forthcoming Laws. This meditative/visualization exercise can continue to benefit you the more you use it. So, once you have done this with the rest of the Laws, you may wish to repeat, once again starting with the Law of Order.

THE LAW OF BALANCE
Latin name is Libra,
The seventh sign of the Zodiac

Everything in the Universe is in constant pursuit of balance. Without balance, there would be chaos. Order and balance are interdependent and work in tandem with each other. So when change occurs it happens in support of order and balance.

For every action there is an equal and opposite reaction, is the scientific aspect of the Law of Balance. The scales of Justice are the symbol of judicial balance. Karma is the action of balance in our Spiritual lives.

Physics is the science of matter and motion. Matter and motion are invariably connected. Without movement, matter could not be. Without matter, there would be nothing to move. We could carry this definition further and say that physics is also the science of order and balance. Without order, matter would be irregular and impossible to study. Without motion, balance could not be created. Recognizing the law of balance in science gives us a deeper understanding of the universe. An example would be in the science of medicine. Western medicine isolates conditions from the whole, believing that disease is an isolated condition created by happenstance. Eastern medicine sees sickness as a reaction to disorder and imbalance within the whole being. Nothing is separate. Thus the concept of

Western medicine makes no sense. The more we can recognize the imbalance of the whole, the more we can understand this universal law.

The Law of Karma is a subsidiary supportive Law to the Laws of Balance and Justice. Karma is the executor of these Laws. Whether our action is 'good' or 'in error,' it causes reaction. Reaction triggers connected indebtedness. Connected Indebtedness is karma. Indebtedness, whether negative or positive, gives opportunity for balance in the energies. It also leads to the realization that we are all one. (The Law of One)

Letting go of trying to control everything in our lives allows us to find peace within. This is balance. Most of us have, at one time or another, tried to force things to happen. We think that if a situation is controlled we can achieve what we desire. Yet the lesson proves that we can control nothing except our growth. If we let go of trying to control life's experiences and instead flow with what life presents to us, we gain peace and tranquility, which is in balance with the universe. Our challenge is to learn to flow with nature rather than trying to control it. This is the Law of Balance.

Everything in our lives is part of an ongoing educational program. The Law of Balance is one of our most important teachers.

If every individual in the universe were totally independent, none of the Universal Laws would make sense and karmic indebtedness could not be. Only in the unity of All does indebtedness make sense. Karmic indebtedness gives us the opportunity of knowing "God" in each of us. It is this indebtedness that calls us back to the earth-plane from the so called death state. If we did not learn, we must repeat the lesson.

Our love affair with automobiles creates an imbalance with nature. If our cars were energy efficient and non-polluting, we would still be in an imbalanced state simply because the planet cannot contain the quantity of vehicles that humanity wants. If everyone had a car there wouldn't be much room to drive them.

Until we change our belief that everything that exists is at our disposal to use however we want no matter the consequences, we will continue in the direction of self destruction. We must recognize this imbalance and change or we will cease to be.

Each of us takes some course of action that creates an imbalance with nature and our lives. Our challenge is to recognize this condition and change our habit of egotistical exploitation.

As an example, some of us feel that we should not have to deal with plastic bags that are torn and dirty. There are more important things to do than deal with plastic bags. After all, we have to make payments on a car that takes us to and from work to make money so we can pay for the car, buy food and pay for the house we mortgaged to the

hilt, etc., etc. A plastic bag is not important when com-
pared to the stability and security of our family. This is the
entrapment that many of us find ourselves in. It is not until
we see that if we don't take responsibility for the plastic
bags in our lives, we will become part of the land fill that
the plastic bags are in. There is an old African-American
folk song that says in part: "We're in the same boat, brother. You rock one end, you go'na rock the other."

If we, as individuals, can change so that we flow with nature, then we may be able to influence others to also take
responsibility for the health of the planet. This then is our
hope. We can only change the world to a more balanced
state by first changing ourselves. One person's enlightenment at a time can save our planet and our species.

Exercise #1:

Think of someone that you believe you harmed. Focus
on the situation that was created which caused you to react
the way you did. As best you can, put aside any guilt feelings and examine why you reacted the way you did.
What motivated you to hurt this person? Was it a reaction
to something that happened in the past that you re-
experienced? Was it a reaction to this person's disrespect
to you that was similar to an episode in your past? Or,
perhaps this person was vulnerable as you were at one

time and you hurt this person because you had been hurt in a similar situation. Next allow yourself to go into meditation. Focus on this person in your past that you hurt and simply ask: "Why did I do that?"

This is the second time I have invited you to look to your past as a way of understanding why you behave the way you do. The reason is that each of us is a product of our past. What we experienced as babies and children dictates our relationships to this day. We are creatures of habit and if we look to our habits of behavior, we gain a greater understanding of ourselves. Then with this understanding, we can replace our negative habits with positive ones.

Exercise #2:

As you completed the exercise involving visualization, meditation and your breath with the Law of Order (exercise #3), now do the same with the Law of Balance.

1. Before meditation, make a list of all the things in your life that represent Balance which gave you a beneficial direction. As an example: A healing in the balancing of energies in a relationship.

2. Then make a second list of all the things that represent Imbalance that took you in the "wrong" direction, such

as a continued negative confrontation with a family member.

3.   Next, go into a meditative state and center your attention on your breath.   Now as you inhale, visualize bringing one of the listed Balances into you through your breath.

4,   Then exhale one of the corresponding Imbalances out of you.   Concentrate on bringing in this Balance and casting out the Imbalance with each breath.   Do this as long as you wish.

Note: Obviously, the longer you visualize this positive Balance coming into you and the negative Imbalance leaving you, the better.   In choosing your 'Balances' and 'Imbalances', please keep in mind that there is no duality, so 'Imbalances' are really illusions.

5.   Repeat this breath meditation exercise daily using a different balance-imbalance combination until you have completed your lists.

THE LAW OF HARMONY

With perfect harmony comes peace. With perfect peace comes enlightenment.

Justice and Harmony are cousins to each other. It is the just harmony of all components that forms a connected whole. Being in concert with all that is in the Universe is being in harmony. When we give illusion power or when we dissociate ourselves from the unity of all things, we create disharmony. Fear is disharmony and is based on illusion. We create illusion because we think in terms of separation not unity. Fear has to do with 'what if' and 'maybe.' All things in the Universe are immortal. What appears as death or destruction is simply change. Change is a vital part of harmony. Yet we fear change because we are insecure about who we are.

When we are in harmony, we see ourselves as extensions of God, as all things are extensions of God. We do not judge anything right or wrong or better or less because everything is of equal value. (We, of course, need to assess whether things or conditions are out of integrity with the Laws, but we should not judge them right or wrong, but simply understand that we are dealing with confusion.) Nothing that exists is different in value. We are in sympathetic association with everything. It is when we are in total acceptance of all that we approach harmony which brings peace to the spirit.

When we think of harmony in music, we think of notes and chords that compliment one another and support the melody and theme. So, also in the universe when we find energies or vibrations that are in a complimentary state to one another, we see the law of harmony in action. When we are in concert with all that is in the universe, we are operating in the law of harmony. The Law of Attraction/Repulsion Is the subsidiary Law of the Law of Harmony. When vibrations are attracted to one another or when vibration are repulsed away from each other, this is the Law of Harmony in action. Gravity or magnets are examples.

When we give illusion power or when we dissociate ourselves from the unity of all things we create disharmony or discord.

I have noticed that some people believe that they have advanced enough that looking and dealing with old issues is not necessary. "Been there, done that." Yet if we wake up in the morning and find ourselves still in our bodies, we probably still have more to do. Ego can be an insidious creature. Understanding that none of us has as yet ascended to any angelic realm, allows us to be more honest and humble.

A man that I had done readings and counseling for came to me distraught. "Why am I always choosing women that are screwed up? Why can't I find someone who can compliment my life?" When I pointed out that he chooses women based on his past experiences of limitation of entitlement and that he needed to go deeper into his past pain to understand this habit, he balked. "Santi, you have no idea (of) how much I have worked on myself. I've done it all, every therapy you can name I've done. So don't tell me I have to explore my past more, I've done that, to the point of exhaustion. I don't need to do that any more." This man has embraced 'victimhood' as his reality and egotistically embraced the trap of complacency.

When we help others, we help ourselves. We teach what we need to learn. All of these observations should be done with loving appreciation for where we have come and where we need to go. But if we get caught in the trap of complacency we become stagnated. We must understand this trap. Any resistance to Spiritual growth is painful. If we understand the teachings of pain it is then that we move toward ascension. Also our attitude toward pain is bound to change into a more appreciated understanding. It is in this understanding that we can move through pain more easily. At some point, we can shift into a greater consciousness so we can learn without pain. This, of-course, comes much later in our growth toward awareness.

So we must look in the mirror of our past pain to gain a better understanding of ourselves. The more we gain a clarity of what our pain has been, the more liberated we become. In order for us to delve into the discomfort of our painful past experiences, we need to acknowledge what will be the benefit of reliving the pain. It is only in understanding the pain that we can be free of it. What were the circumstances of the pain? Who were the ones that inflicted the pain? Can we understand their pain and why they passed it on and why we accepted the pain? Once we can answer these questions we can feel ourselves in the Law of Harmony.

Exercise #1:

In this exercise you will need a timer and a commitment of 15 minutes a day for 30 days. It involves a mantra/ chant that will empower you to move even closer to your Spiritual truth. It is designed to awaken you to reality.

If at first the mantra/chant seems uncomfortable, this is because you have been separated too long from the truth. It is unfamiliar territory. So, for this exercise to work, please be patient. Keeping in mind that because most of us have spent our entire lives believing the opposite, the commitment to 30 days is necessary.

1. Designate an area in your home for this exercise. Make sure that your chanting won't be disturbing to others. Set a time (preferably in the morning) that you can be consistent with. If, for some reason, you miss a day, then do

30 minutes the next day. The idea is to be persistent.

2.   Sit in a comfortable chair or couch and set your timer for 15 minutes, then chant the following out loud or silently to yourself, over and over:

"I am One very Beautiful Human
being Order, Balance and Harmony."

After your 30 day commitment, you may wish to continue. The more you are involved with this mantra/chant the more you will experience a shift in your appreciation of self. This is very subtle and you may not notice any immediate change because of this, but you will change. The more you are with this affirmation, the more you will realize your value. Also, having read and experienced the Laws of Order and Balance, this chant also helps you to be aware of these Laws as well.

Exercise #2:

Imagine that you have decided to move to the country. You want to build a log cabin and live near a stream or lake. After much searching, you find the ideal piece of land and you buy it. After a year of planning and building, you have your home. You have water from your well and electricity from solar panels and a wind generator. What has also been your dream was to grow all your fruits and vegetables and raise chickens, so you build a green-house and a chicken coop. You also lay out a flat piece of land for a large garden. You start your garden with corn, peas, beans and squash. In your green-house you plant grapes, tomatoes, lettuces, cucumbers and strawberries. For your chickens, you plant a small field of flax, alfalfa and clover. You have planned everything very well except for one small detail.

Every other animal in the country appreciates your gift to them and they come to help you harvest everything. The foxes are quite grateful to you for giving them your chickens. The mice, chipmunks, squirrels, racoons and deer want to thank you for everything in your garden and green-house.

Yet there is nothing left for you. What do you do? Do you set out traps? Do you leave poison out? What would you do to secure your food? Keep in mind that this exercise has to do with being in harmony with yourself and nature. Please take your time to answer these questions so that you can create a harmony between yourself and all the other animals in the forest. This dilemma, in the larger picture, is what humanity must resolve to bring us into the Law of Harmony not only with the other animals of our planet but our fellow humans.

Exercise #3:

As you completed the exercise involving visualization, meditation and your breath with the Law of Balance, now do the same with the Law of Harmony.

1. Before meditation, make a list of all the things in your life that represents Harmony which gave you a beneficial direction. As an example: Clarity you obtained in the direction you want to go in in life.

2. Then make a second list of all the things that represent Disharmony that took you in the 'wrong' direction. Such as, a fear of failing at something.

3. Next, go into a meditative state and center your attention on your breath. Now as you inhale visualize bringing one of the listed Harmonies into you through your breath. Then exhale one of the corresponding Disharmonies out of you. Concentrate on bringing in this Harmony and casting out the Disharmony with each breath. Do this as long as you wish.

Note: Obviously, the longer you visualize this positive Harmony coming into you and the negative Disharmony leaving you the better. In choosing your 'Harmonies' and 'Disharmonies,' please keep in mind that there is no duality so 'Disharmonies' are really illusions.

4.   Repeat this breath meditation exercise daily using a different harmony-disharmony combination until you have completed your lists.

As I said before, this exercise will be more powerful and beneficial to you the more you use it.

Exercise #4:

This exercise involves the Laws of Order, Balance and Harmony.

Pick three objects from nature that you feel connected to. As an example, let us say you pick a rock, stick and feather. Now ask yourself to identify each of the three laws in each of the three objects. In other words: How is the Law of Order, Balance and Harmony exemplified in the rock, stick and feather?
The second part of this exercise is to identify and explain how each of your objects is interconnected and interdependent to each other. This will require some patience with yourself, yet doing this part of the exercise will make it easier for you to understand the first three Laws and subsequently the rest of the Laws.

THE LAW OF GROWTH

*Karma is the executing force for opportunity of growth.
Once we become conscious of cause and effect we can
move away from ignorance and grow.*

The universe is in a constant state of change and expansion. Whether this condition shifts and either stops expanding or reverses direction, we do not know at this time. Yet the movement of expansion is under the dictates of the Law of Growth. My guess would be that if we shift into a state of contraction, the law of growth would shift into a contractual law. In other words growth would be created by contraction. My suspicion, however, is that we will continue to expand.

The continuous change of everything is a partial definition of growth. Yet there is much more to growth than change. Growth has to do with the continuance and expansion of awareness or consciousness within everything. Changes are stages in the process of the opportunities for the acquisition of consciousness. A mystic once said that even rocks breathe and that for us to see rocks breathing is to let go of time. My read of this is that all things have a consciousness. The complete awareness of one's own consciousness can only be achieved when the individual can see a rock breathe. Solidness that we attribute to rocks is illusion. There is space between all molecules as well as movement within each molecule. So if there is space and movement, then how do we define solidness?

There are some who can decorporate. (The word decorporate comes from Spirit. Corporate means combined into one body; united or grouped together. Decorporate then means to separate the body. That is to separate their cells and their molecular structure so that they can pass through 'solid' objects such as walls.) Another word for this is dematerialization. But to be able to do this takes an enormous consciousness and understanding of self and to feel the molecular world. Yet, there are Master Forces in the universe that can do just that. We have been told that Jesus as a young man of 19 was able to do this. Yet Jesus tells us that he only did this once, after the crucifixion.* When we gain an expanded consciousness with All, we have the opportunity to become unlimited.

To know that a seed needs soil and water to grow, is one truth. To know that without love the seed could not germinate and grow, no matter how rich the soil or abundant the water, is to know the greater truth. Yet, the greater truth still, is that all seeds have love inherently present within or they would not be. So it is with the seed of humanity. Love is the product of Growth and Growth is the product of Love

---

* Talks With Christ, page 129

30

and this brings the opportunity for the expansion of consciousness and Illumination.

Having no activity toward expanded consciousness is the opposite of growth. If we are not moving toward a greater understanding of ourselves and the universe, we are stagnant.

I know of a social worker who has been a tremendous help to people. He is a very loving person and would do most anything to help those in need. Yet he lives in a kind of stagnation of spirit. His ego presents a false image to others and himself that he rarely makes mistakes, his wisdom is beyond reproach and his anger is always justified. There is a hidden part of him that he does not acknowledge. I believe it has to do with an imbalance between his masculine and feminine sides. He grew up without the needed support of a father and had to make his way through life on his own. What he accomplished, without the support of his father, is very creditable and commendable. Yet this lack of support prevented him from letting go of the control his ego has on him. So in spite of all that he has accomplished, he is spiritually handicapped. If only he could see the deeper side of his controlling ego, perhaps he could make a breakthrough. There is always hope.

I feel that all of us, at one time or another, have had a similar relationship with our egos. It is kind of like wearing a pair of old shoes that are very comfortable and yet has a nail sticking into our sole (or soul). We ignore the nail's discomfort because we like the comfort of the old shoes. What we do not realize is that a new pair of shoes would be much more comfortable without the nail.

Life can be simple, easy and always peaceful if we let go of ego control. My understanding from Spirit is that the earth-plane is the hardest school in the entire universe because of the ego's resistance to let go of control. When we can feel and thus know that we all are united as one we can bring a growth toward peace. Each of us, who has elected to be here, is blessed with the opportunity for quantum leaps in our Spiritual growth. We just need to take advantage of these opportunities when we sense them. So the more comfort we can have in looking at habitual patterns of behavior to see what part the ego plays, the better.

Exercise #1:

In this exercise I invite you to use your imagination once more. Go into a meditative state while envisioning yourself as an angel with the multitude of like beings, such as Jesus, Mohammed, Moses, Buddha, Krishna and such. Think of yourself as being on an equal state of consciousness with them. They accept you as one of them. In this state of comradery, one of these Masters asks you how you gained your angelic state. In your imagination, create a story that embraces credibility as a plausible path that you took. Take your time with this story. Embellish each part of your journey with as much detail as you can. Make this a Hollywood motion picture story with you playing the lead role.

When you feel complete with the story, return to the conscious state and ponder your 'motion picture.' What were the road blocks that you discovered as you related your story? How did you overcome these road blocks? Can you identify what your road blocks are in this life from your story? In your imaginary path to the angelic realm, do you see where you need to go in your next step toward enlightenment? The answers you give yourself can lead you to a new path to take in your Spiritual Growth. Congratulations.

Exercise #2:

In Buddhism: "The techniques for proceeding to enlightenment are called the path, which is set forth in stages to clarify the order of their practice, ranging from what a beginner should do on up to the ultimate attainment of perfection."** This quote is an excellent definition of the Law of Growth.

** Becoming Enlightened, by the Dalai Lama, page 13

In looking at your pathway, can you recognize the stages of your growing awareness that helped to give you direction? Take time to quiz yourself into remembering the times that you had learned to shift into a new more positive path. Write down, in your own short-hand, those times of revelation.

Now review the stages and the Interval between each stage to see how you progressed. Can you see how each interval moved you Into the next stage of awareness? Understanding this progression may now give you more insight into your pathway to illumination. This review should help you see the pathway of your continuous journey.

Exercise #3:

In the same way you completed the exercises involving visualization, meditation and your breath in the previous Laws, now do the same with the Law of Growth.

1. Before meditation, make a list of all the things in your life that represents Growth which gave you a beneficial direction. As an example: A shift from confusion in your awareness of yourself to the truth of who you are. Or it could have been a shock that forced you to reevaluate yourself.

2. Then make a second list of all the things that repre-

sent stagnation that took you in the "wrong" direction. Such as, the illusion of security in the status quo.

3.   Next, go into a meditative state and center your attention on your breath.   Now as you inhale, visualize bringing one of the listed Growths in through your breath. Then exhale one of the corresponding Stagnations out. Concentrate on bringing in this Growth and casting out the Stagnation with each breath. Do this as long as you wish.

Note: Obviously, the longer you visualize this positive Growth coming in and the negative Stagnation leaving, the better.

4.   Repeat this breath meditation exercise daily using a different growth-stagnation combination until you have completed your lists. As I said before, this exercise will be more powerful and beneficial to you the more you use it.

THE LAW OF APPRECIATION
OR GOD PERCEPTION
(The Law of One)

"When thou knowest Love, then shalt thou know that neither thou, nor giant sun, nor blade of grass can say the words "I am alone I," for in my Father's house there is but ONE, and that ONE He, and thee, and me."

The Message of the Divine Iliad, volume II -by Walter Russell, cir. 1949. Used with permission by the publisher, University of Science and Philosophy, Swannanoa Waynesboro, Virginia.

When we can see the validity in the interconnections and interdependences of everything, then we can realize the truth of the Law of One. Everything is One or if you wish, everything is God.

With the perception of God comes the realization of the equality of all things. If a molecule is an extension of God and a galaxy is an extension of God, how can one be more important than the other? Can any part of God be greater than another? If so, who is qualified to judge this? If a galaxy contains innumerable quantities of molecules, does not this demand that we say that the galaxy is more important? The assumption is that there is a limitation in God. If God is unlimited, then numbers have no meaning, and if numbers have no meaning, then one molecule is as valuable as a galaxy.

Once we begin to see God as all, from the smallest known subatomic particle to the largest known cluster of galaxies, we begin to understand the Law of One. That time and space have meaning or even exist is the question that faces not only the physicist but the Spiritual seeker as well. But we must do more than just see God. We must feel Her/Him externally and internally.

When we view ourselves as being a separate individual, that is a truth. When we also view ourselves as being part of the whole (humanity), this is also truth. But when we come to the realization that we are all part of the whole and therefore cannot be separated, we have come to the greater truth. Molecules are separate individuals, yet without their neighbors they could not exist. It is the electro-magnetic interactions between molecules that creates the dependency. So everything in the universe is connected and interdependent. Separation is illusion.

We are connected and dependent on each other. Democrats and Republicans, conservatives and liberals, Jews and Muslims, Hindus and Christians, atheists and agnostics: we are all brothers and sisters to each other. All of us want the same things; food, shelter, security, love, understanding and respect. So why the illusion of separation? We fear each other because we do not feel this connection. In this illusion, we egotistically believe that we are superior. It was in this illusionary, insecure, angry state that the white Southerner was able to justify slavery. It is not until we as individuals can understand that to love thy neighbor as thyself is the greater truth and until we live this truth, we cannot become liberated from the fear that separates us.

If you desire power or enlightenment, then you must be close to God, which is the source of all power and knowing. Being close to God means understanding and feeling from your heart that you and God are one. Dictators have the illusion of having power because, out of fear, it is given to them, but real power can only come from God. If the ego is behind the motivation for power, then the connection to God is lost and all the power that the person has comes from fear, which has no foundation in truth. Power (or enlightenment) can only come to those who divorce themselves from the negative addiction of the ego for control. It is the difference between belief and knowing.

In 1959 Carl Jung was asked to appear on the BBC program *Face to Face*. John Freeman, the presenter, asked if he believed in God, Jung replied "Believe? Hard to say. I know."

May we all <u>know</u> God.

Exercise #1:

If you have a favorite crystal, you will want to use it in this exercise. If you do not have a favorite crystal, then go outside and look for a rock that strikes your fancy.

Place your crystal or rock on a table and sit in front of it. Make sure that you are comfortable. Concentrate and focus on your crystal or rock. Quiet your mind and allow your concentration to be absolute. Be patient with this exercise and give yourself unlimited time to "feel" the rock or crystal. Without giving you any suggestions, at some point you will feel a connection with your "friend." This is a form of meditation and as such it will only work when you remove yourself from as much thought as possible. Also, if you allow yourself to send love to your friend, this will help to bridge the connection.

We are potentially unlimited in our ability to feel life in all things. It is up to us to experience this life in so called inanimate objects which allows us to go into a higher realm of consciousness. As unusual as this exercise may seem, it can be enormously beneficial. So be patient and allow the stone or crystal to make the connection, not you. Once you feel a oneness with your friend, then you will be connected. It is at this point that your 'friend' may wish to share thoughts, observations and/or love. Communication can take many forms. Listen with your heart, not your ears.

You may need to do this several times in order for you to

connect. So please be patient with yourself. The more you move toward a connection, the more apt you are in feeling the aliveness of your crystal or rock.

Exercise #2:

Everything that was created those billions of years ago has since been in a constant flux toward expanded consciousness. The evolution of the cosmos is a testament to the perfection of God's creative energies. The more that we can see and feel this goal toward total consciousness, the more peace we will have about our own evolution. This exercise has to do with you becoming more aware of the consciousness of all things. Another thing to think about is, can there be a difference between consciousness and intelligence? Just because an individual is intelligent, this does not mean that there is an expanded consciousness. Most tyrants are certainly intelligent but I do not think that they are very conscious. Having said this, I believe it would be a bit presumptuous for me to assume that I or anyone else could prove to you that everything is growing toward expanded consciousness. Yet in quantum physics, there is growing evidence of a consciousness in the most minute particle. Each of us can 'feel' this truth if we allow ourselves to feel the love that exists in the interconnection and the interdependence of one thing to another.

What we are dealing with is a feeling of the truth not needing intellectual or scientific proof. So my invitation to you is to trust the wisdom of your feeling in this exercise and temporarily ignore your logical and rational thinking. After the exercise, you can compare your two types of knowings and wisdoms.

Go for a walk in a park or forest. Stop when you find a comfortable place to sit. Look around on the ground until you find an insect. Watch the insect and where it is going. Does its activity make any sense to you? If not, pay closer attention to this insect and see if you can understand its behavior. Why is it moving in the direction it is going? Think of yourself as a scientist whose job is to study the behavior of this insect. It must be obvious that your insect has intelligence or it could not be independently moving. The question to be with is: Does my insect friend have a sense of self? Does it have an awareness of its environment? When you place your hand in front of its path, does it go over or around your hand? What level of awareness do you feel your insect friend has in order to make a decision as to which path to take to move away from the obstacle of your hand? I am asking you to ponder not only the intelligence of the insect but also whether there is any indication of a consciousness within the animal. It is more than likely moving in search of food, shelter or a mate. So what level of consciousness can you see that may be involved in the insect's activity, if any?

Let us explore your insect's history. Millions, perhaps billions of years ago, it was of a different design than what it has evolved into. In your imagination can you see that it has become more evolved over the millenniums of time? And in this evolution would you not expect that the individual would become more conscious? Does not sophistication hint at the presence of consciousness? Perhaps not. Yet, perhaps so. What _feels_ right to you?

Exercise #3:

In the same way you completed the exercise involving visualization, meditation and your breath, now do the same with the Law of Appreciation.

1. Before meditation, make a list of all the things in your life that gave you an appreciation of yourself and how this appreciation may have expanded into a different view of God. As an example: You may have discovered a truthful part of yourself that you admire and were unconscious of before and this brought you into a deeper love of God.

2. Then make a second list of all the things that represent a feeling of separation, isolation or rejection.

3.   Next, go into a meditative state and center your attention on your breath.   Now as you inhale, visualize bringing one of the listed self appreciations into yourself through your breath.   Then exhale out one of the corresponding rejections you may have experienced.   Do this as long as you wish.

Obviously, the longer you re-experience this self appreciation coming into you and the negative rejection leaving you, the better.

4.   Repeat this breath meditation exercise daily using a different appreciation-rejection combination until you have completed your lists.

THE LAW OF LOVE
"Love is lord of truth and loyalty." – Edmund Spenser

Love is a feeling; a feeling of a strong connection that commands admiration and delight. Love is brought about by sympathetic vibrations and understanding. So the concept of John Keely's 'Sympathetic Vibratory Physics' can be called the Law of Love.*

Everything in the universe has a vibration. I like to refer to vibration as the pulse of God and the pulse of God as love. So in my definition, vibration is love. Since everything has a vibration, then everything is vibrating in the law of Love. We humans and other animals seem to be the only ones that have the capacity to be angry or hateful. This is a trait that is characteristic of insecurity. So it is only logical that when we are angry or involved in hate we have divorced ourselves momentarily from everything. Anger and hate are products of the ego's inability to see and feel the interdependence and interconnections of all things. Once we begin to feel the interactions of all things, we gain the opportunity to let go of fear and feel love.

Love is the gift without expectation. When we give undonditionally, we are expressing the Law of Spiritual

---

* For more information on John Keely's work contact: "Delta Spectrum Research, Pond Science Institute," 921 Santa Fe Avenue, La Junta, CO 81050 or dalesvp@centurytel.net, or www.svpvril.com

Love. When we give something with the hope that we will receive praise or thanks, this is not love but manipulation. Defining love cannot be as without hate or anger, but must incorporate a heart connection. It is the challenge of us all to be in the oneness of everything, for it is in feeling the oneness that Love can grow. Awareness then has to do with experiencing love, love of all things.

Hate is a feeling, as is love. Yet most of us prefer the joy of love over the expression of hate. Anger is an emotion of reaction. Hate is an emotion of belief. Hitler's hatred for the Jews was based on a belief in their inferiority and interference. His anger was toward anyone who countered this belief.

Any differences in beliefs of peoples can generate hate if there is not understanding. If we are indifferent to others, we welcome misunderstanding and ignorance.

Slavery was an institution of indifference. Africans were used as an economic work force for the promotion of wealth and affluence for the white community. The concept that the white man was superior to the black man came about because of ignorance, arrogance, indifference and economical opportunity. In order for slavery to be justified, the white population had to convince themselves that they were right in their assessment of their superiority. It was not until the rebellions of Nat Turner, John Brown and many others both white and black that the white community began to change their concept of reality. However it was a long, painful and bloody road before we became liberated in the equality of races. (There are, of course, those who still hang onto the illusion of superiority, as there are still those who believe that the world is flat.) It was love that conquered indifference, hate and anger. It was a hard lesson for us all. May we not forget the Hitlers of the world, nor the Dr. Martin Luther King Juniors.

O Fairy Song of Love Everlasting! Rock me in thy cradle of melody and bring me sleep on Her bosom of peace. — *Paramahansa Yogananda*

"Thou shalt love thy neighbor as thyself."
— *Matt. xxii, 39*

Exercise #1:

In this exercise, I am inviting you to define the different kinds of Love that we are aware of. So, for the tools, you will need a pad of paper and a pen.

The different kinds of love are:

1. Mate
2. Family
3. Friend

4. Material

5. Spiritual

6. Physical

7. Planetary and Cosmic

8. Country

9. Self

10. All Life.

1. In your own words, define love of your Mate. Take all the time that you need to be complete with this personal definition. The more accurate your definition, the easier it will be to define the other types of love.

2. Next, define Family Love and again expand on how this love feels to you.

3. What is friendship love?

4. How do you define material Love?

5. Now define Spiritual love. If you are an atheist, then your definition would probably center around logic, reason and an appreciation for pragmatism. If you are involved with a religion, then your definition would probably center around that.

6. Now define physical love. This should include love of

sex, food, sports, study and anything pleasurable that has to do with our mind and body. Again, if there is an imbalance with other loves, then there is probably conflict.

7. In defining planetary and cosmic love, think of how you feel when you look at the stars at night. If you are like me, you may long to go into space and explore. Yet, it is knowing how profoundly we are connected to the universe that allows us to be there.

8. Next, define love of country. Is your definition relegated to ethnicity, region or government? Is your love of country in conflict with your love of the human race?

9. Define the love you have for yourself.

10. Explore how you feel towards all life on this planet and elsewhere. This feeling could be defined as love of life.

In your definitions, is there anything about your relationship with money or material things that may feel in conflict with your spiritual direction? Do either of these types of love control you? Is there any confusion involved in how you define either of these loves? These are not easy questions to answer, but you may find an awareness of the relationship you have with the material and money being in conflict with your spiritual direction. Perhaps not. My contention is that there should be a balance between the material and the Spiritual for there to be peace.

Exercise #2:

This is an exercise that you do first thing in the morning. Before you go to the toilet or have coffee, walk over to the mirror, look at your reflection, smile at yourself and say the following out loud:

"I love me, I respect me and I cherish the perfection that I am."

What this exercise does is to set the foundation of love for your relationship with yourself for the whole day. What most of us do in the morning is look in the mirror, frown and say something to the effect: "God what a mess I am. I've got to put my makeup on before anyone sees me." Or "Good Lord, I look terrible, I need a shave and fix my messy hair." What we do in these cases is create a negative relationship with ourselves that lasts the whole day and spills over into our relationship with others. We place greater value on how we think we appear to others than the truth of who we are.

Exercise #3:

In the same way that you did the exercises involving visualization, meditation and your breath in the previous Laws, now do the same with the Law of Love.

1. Before meditation, make a list of all the things in your life that represent your experiences with the different types of Love in your life. As an example: Your experiences with love of Mother Earth or a place on Mother Earth, type of food, job, a love of a person, relative, offspring, pets, etc.

2. Then make a second list of all the situations or persons that you have hated (or still do), or resent or who bring to you sadness or anger.

3. Next, go into a meditative state and center your attention on your breath. Now as you inhale, visualize bringing one of the listed Loves into yourself through your breath. Then exhale one of the corresponding negatives out. Concentrate on the bringing in this Love and casting out the negative with each breath. Do this as long as you wish. Obviously, the longer you visualize this positive Love coming into you and the negative leaving you, the better.

4. Repeat this breath meditation exercise daily using a different love-anger combination until you have completed your lists.

THE LAW OF COMPASSION

"The more we develop compassion,
the more genuinely ethical our conduct will be."
–His Holiness the XIV Dalai Lama

Compassion is choosing to feel empathy in fellowship with another. Identifying with another's misfortune and understanding their pain is compassion. The larger picture of compassion is being aware that the individual has created the condition of misfortune and pain, yet still having empathy for their condition.

Love and Compassion are completely related. They cannot be separated. Compassionate feelings are love in action. Love is the seed for Compassion to blossom. Compassion is the flower that gives seed to Love.

Compassion is the culmination of God's first six Laws. It is the Law of these Laws. When we vibrate with Order, Balance, Harmony, Growth, Oneness and Love, we vibrate in the Law of Compassion. When we can see and appreciate beauty in all things in God's creation, then we live in the Law of Compassion. Truth is a manifestation of Compassion and Love. Sympathetic commiseration is Compassion. So developing a compassionate attitude gives opportunity for enlightenment and peace.

Our challenge is to feel a connection with others. This is not easy to do when we are convinced that we are right in our evaluation of reality. It is not until our fear dissipates enough to sense the pain of others, that we can make a shift in our consciousness to compassion.

When we recognize that there are only two emotions in the universe, love and fear, we can move toward our liberation. Of the two emotions only one is based on truth. All fear is based on illusion. Yet facing our fear can help us toward liberation if we understand that it is pointing in the direction we need to go. If we are a slave to fear, then love has no room in our lives, let alone compassion. It is not until we champion our fears through understanding, that we can begin to feel compassion for others.

"The true path is being and living a humble, compassionate love for even the very oxygen that you inhale within your lungs, and for the spirituality within every individual."
    – From "The God Within"
    by Elwood Babbitt and Charles Hapgood

"The realization that we are all basically the same human beings, who seek happiness and try to avoid suffering, is very helpful in developing a sense of brotherhood and sisterhood, a warm feeling of love and compassion for others."
    – His Holiness the XIV Dalai Lama

Note: Any book written by His Holiness the Dalai Lama is based on the Law of Compassion.

Exercise #1:

To do this exercise my suggestion would be for you to record the following and then play it back to yourself once you are in meditation. Have your recording machine close by so that when you turn it on you will not disturb your meditative state.

Picture yourself In Ethiopia. You are surrounded with a mass of humanity. Mothers with babies, old couples, disfigured and broken bodies. All of them starving, sick and in varying stages of dying. The babies have protruding stomachs, flies covering their mouths and eyes. They are listless trying to suckle their mothers dry breast. There is no water and the temperature is 115 degrees Fahrenheit. (Pause)

You see a little girl who is about 10 or 12 years old with her little brother in her arms. She is sitting on the ground off of the pathway that leads from the desert. Asking her where her parents are, she tells you that their mother and father are dead. They were killed by military troops that invaded her village. When they came into her village, she grabbed her brother and hid in a dry gully. After the soldiers left she did not know what to do so she followed the trail to this abandoned village where she thought there would be food and water and someone to take them in. She and her brother had walked for three days and part of the night. She was afraid of the night because of the animals and she was afraid of the day because of the soldiers. She started to cry and could not stop. No one paid her any attention except you. (Pause)

In the area, that was once a water hole, there is an abandoned truck. You have been told that there is a town about one hundred miles away where you could get food and water. Yet the road is used by the military. What do you decide to do to help the little girl and the other people? (Pause)

Do you go for help alone? Do you try to load the people into the truck to take them to the town or do you ignore the situation and move on? Explore all the possibilities that you can think of. (Pause)

Now allow yourself to return to a conscious state and review what course of action you took. Granted it is difficult to determine what you would do in a real situation like this, but, this should give you an idea of where you stand with the Law of Compassion.

Exercise #2

All of us at one time or another have believed that someone has hurt us. Choose a person that you believe has hurt you in the past. As best you can, divorce yourself from the memory of the pain. This may be hard to do but it is onlyin your developed attitude of a dispassionate observer that this exercise will have value. Ask yourself:

1. 'What was the cause behind the attack on me?'
2. 'What was going on with this person?'

Give yourself ample time to consider all the different possibilities. When someone seems to cause pain, the reasons are often hidden quite deeply. The more you can discover what was going on with that person on this deeper level, the easier it will be for you to understand what the motivation was. When we have a better understanding of the person's motivation, we can begin to understand that person's pain. It more often than not has to do with a lack of respect, appreciation, understanding and love.

With this new understanding of the person who you believe hurt you, do you have a different feeling toward this person than you did before this exercise? Please examine what your feelings are and see if you can identify and name your feelings now. If, in your discovery, the feeling of compassion appears then this exercise has given you a greater appreciation of yourself.

Exercise #3:

In the same way that you completed the exercises involving visualization, meditation and your breath in the previ-

ous Laws, now do the same with the Law of Compassion.

1. Before meditation, make a list of all the times you re-member when you felt compassion. As an example: You may have felt a strong reaction to the holocaust, or to starving children in Ethiopia.

2. Then make a second list of all the situations or per-sons that you felt indifferent to.

3. Next, go into a meditative state and center your at-tention on your breath. Now as you inhale, visualize bringing compassion for any individual or group on your list into yourself through your breath. Then exhale one of the corresponding negative indifferent attitudes out. Con-centrate on bringing in this compassion and casting out the negative with each breath. Do this as long as you wish.

Obviously, the longer you visualize this compassion coming in and the negative leaving, the better.

4. Repeat this breath meditation exercise daily using a different compassion-indifference combination until you have completed your lists.

THE ABSENT LAWS OF VISHNU
(GOD)

The next five Laws are ones that are not actively present on the Earth Plane at this time. They are goals for us to reach. Truth, Justice, Mercy, Salvation and Illumination are the Laws that can liberate humanity into inner peace. Two things we have to develop: One, we must feel a unity with the first seven Laws, and two, we must develop a loving understanding and compassion toward all others and all things in a continuum. This, of course, does not mean that we ignore these five laws until we feel a unity of the first seven. On the contrary, the more that we strive toward them the more we solidify our unity and understanding of all the laws.

The reason that these five are not active on the Earth Plane is that most of humanity operates in opposition to them. We tend to embrace, lying, injustice, savage disregard, victimization and separation as our illusionary reality.

Even though these Laws are not universally active on the Earth Plane, that does not mean they cannot be active within each of us. The more we become conscious of our relationship with them, the greater the opportunity we create for their reactivation. So by being in integrity with these laws individually, we help move all of humanity into greater enlightenment and peace.

THE LAW OF TRUTH

"Truth is the expanded Ring of All Creativity."
-Lochia, Teacher of Christ*

There are four types of Truth:

1, Actual or Empirical Truth is learned through observation or experiment.

2, Logical Truth Is when certain premises give a certain conclusion. These are sometimes called necessary truths.

3, Ethical Truth is based on value judgement or assessment.

4, Metaphysical or Spiritual Truth is based on expanded consciousness of reality, conceived by perceived actuality and experience.

1.   Present awareness defines *Actual or Empirical Truth.* The truth in physics is that there are gases, liquids, solids, and plasma that make up the universe. The truth in quantum physics is that defining gases, liquids, solids, and plasma is meaningless. Both are correct, both speak the truth and both base their truth upon differing degrees of awareness. Another example is that once humanity thought women were the emotional beings and men the logical, rational ones. For society, at that time, this was

_____

*Talks With Christ, page 150

true. However the awareness level has changed. So now the truth is that both sexes are logical, pragmatic and emotional and neither has a rigid monopoly on either. Still, there are some who now believe that women are more pragmatic and men are more emotional. I sense that the sexes are becoming more balanced in both areas. The sexes, of course, remain different, but it is the definitions of character that have changed the perception of truth. The difference is:

Men swoon to mate,
Women womb create.

Each individual, whether male or female, needs to experience life in both sexes. In order for a male to experience being female, and a female being male, there is a need for one or more transitional lives to occur. This is why homosexuality exists. Painful as these transitional lives may be, they are a gift to us all so that we can appreciate and understand male and female forms of God's creation of humanity. So when we encounter a homosexual or lesbian person, we need to understand that they are committed to experiencing the opposite sex for Spiritual expansion and should be praised and honored.

2. *Logical Truth* is conformity to fact or reality, yet fact and reality change with consciousness. So we must look at truth as an ongoing redefining of fact and reality. Truth is

defined in the moment. It reveals itself in degrees of awareness. The greater the awareness, the greater the truth. The highest truth is achieved when there is complete awareness of ALL.

3. *Ethical Truth* is from or relates to moral action, motive or character. Ethics is founded in honesty. So ethical truth is honesty in action. This truth demands integrity and freedom from fraud and corruption. When we lie, even "white" lies, we are out of integrity with ethical truth.

4. *Metaphysical or Spiritual Truth* comes to us when we trust the wisdom of our intuition. It is acknowledging our psychic abilities (which everyone has) as our best guide to truth. The greatest truth is the Law of One. When we can acknowledge that everything is of equal value because everything comes from one source, then we are in integrity with the law of Spiritual Truth. If we judge one thing or person as having more value than another, then I would suggest that this realization comes from ego or a false sense of superiority, not truth. Who has the right or ability to judge value in the universe? Everything is different by design and nature. Still all things are of equal value.

Everything is ruled by the *Law of Truth*. All of the other *Laws* are subservient to truth. It is not until each of us can be completely honest and truthful that we can begin to achieve peace and enlightenment. It has been said that the *Laws of Justice and Mercy* are subservient to the *Law of Truth*.** Because it is truth that allows Justice and Mercy to prevail.

Lying seems to be a natural conditional reflex for all of us to use when we feel the need to protect our egos and others egos or to give ourselves a better or more important Illusionary image. Two words that are always associated with lies are: Embellishment and exaggeration. Lies are also a way of hiding from reality. If we are to move into the higher realms of consciousness we need to champion our fears and let go of our lies. To tell the truth, even when the truth seems to hurt us, is our challenge. We need to develop a courageous, committed attitude to honesty that will vanquish our fears. This is our challenge, to see that truth can do no harm.

There is an old Latin saying: *En Vino, Veritas*, In wine there is truth. In other words when we let go of control and inhibitions (fear) we become more truthful. Also, when we dare to doubt or question, we are lead to truth.

** Talks With Christ, pages 153 & 154

"The better definition is this: correlate those truths that are enacted in each and every dream that becomes a part of the entity of the individual and use such (for the purpose of) better development; ever remembering that 'develop' means going TOWARD the higher forces, or the Creator."

- Edgar Cayce (3744-4)

Jesus said:

"Blessed is the wise person who seeks truth. When one finds it, one rests upon it forever, and is not afraid of those who want to disturb one."

-Chapter 4:13, The Gnostic Gospel of the Book of Thomas from the Nag Hammadi Library.

"Truth is exact correspondence with reality."
-Paramahansa Yogananda

Exercise #1:

This exercise is designed to bring clarity to your habitual patterns of lying. It is not about judgement. The exercise is designed to make you aware of this conditional reflex that we all are involved with. Acknowledging that you lie is the first step. Do not beat yourself up because you have not achieved perfection. Lighten up. Okay?

We lie for a number of reasons: One, we may be embarrassed with the truth or, two, we are afraid of getting hurt or hurting someone else. Lying gives us a false sense of security and comfort. Once we begin to move away from lying, we can see and feel a liberation of our spirit.

1. Carry a note pad with you as you start your day. Whenever you catch yourself lying, write it in your note pad. That evening look over what you recorded and ask yourself; "What would have happened if I had told the truth?" Would the truth have created a condition that would seem to have hurt you or someone else?

2. Close your eyes and go over the incident and imagine yourself telling the truth. Now imagine the reaction to your honesty. This is what your fear has told you would happen if you did not lie.

3. Next imagine the reaction differently. See yourself

being in integrity with the truth and let your attitude be lovingly supportive of everyone involved. What was the consequence of your honesty?   You may be surprised with what you experience in your imagination.

Developing an uncomfortable attitude toward lying is the first step toward liberating yourself from this habit. It is replacing one habit of behavior with a more positive one. We all have the ability to conquer our fear. Being truthful creates a quantum leap In living in illumination, if we are lovingly persistent with ourselves. The path to enlightenment can only be reached in a loving relationship
with ourselves.

Exercise #2:

As you did in the exercises involving visualization, meditation and your breath in the previous Laws, now do the same with the Law of Truth.

1. Before meditation, make a list of all the times that you remember when you were compelled to be truthful in spite of your fear. As an example: As a child you may have confessed to stealing cookies that your mother had baked knowing that you might be punished.

2. Then make a second list of the times that you remem-

ber lying.

3. Next, go into a meditative state and center your attention on your breath. Now, as you inhale, visualize bringing that truth into yourself through your breath. Then exhale one of the corresponding lies that you told. Concentrate on the bringing in this truth and casting out the negative lie with each breath. Do this as long as you wish. The longer you visualize the truth coming in and the lie leaving you, the better.

4. Repeat this breath meditation exercise daily using a different truth-lie combination until you have completed your lists.

THE LAW OF JUSTICE

To be just is to act with compassionate understanding.

Our current attempt at justice is found in our judicial system. We create laws to guide us toward harmony with each other and when these are violated, we activate our judicial system to bring a balance of justice to the one violated and the violator. For now, it is the best system we have. Yet, the law of justice is only effective to the degree of consciousness of our society, the judge, the court and jury. As a result, we often find ourselves occupied with vengeance rather than justice. We will continue to handicap ourselves until we understand that justice comes only when we have a deeper understanding of cause and effect.

The *Law of Cause and Effect (Karma)* is the *Law of Justice* in the embryonic state. *Karma* is the executor of the *Laws of Balance* and *Justice*. Whether our action is attuned to reality or illusion (fear), it causes reaction. Reaction triggers connected indebtedness. Connected indebtedness is karma. Indebtedness, whether negative or positive, gives opportunity for balance in the energies. The Law of Justice can only apply when there is a balance of harmony between what an individual has caused and what the effects have been. Justice, then, also has to do with the *Laws of Balance and Harmony*.

Concerning the *Law of One*; there cannot be justice upon the earth plane, or anywhere else, without equality and impartiality imbued within the consciousness of those involved. When we divorce ourselves from prejudice, embrace a grain of sand as our brother, view all with equality and, alas, ourselves as part of all, no more or less than the grain of sand or an angel, then we flow with justice.

The Jains believe in the sacredness of all life. Yet, to believe that you have failed yourself by 'accidentally' stepping on an ant, is not being just to the harmony of nature. If you choose to step on an ant for no other reason than to destroy, then you are in disharmony and are being unjust to God and yourself.

Flowing with nature gives cause to justice. Going against nature brings disharmony, imbalance and disorder. You then become unjust. When you can truthfully say that you had no intended ill effect upon any living creature or thing, including yourself, then you will have lived in the *Law of Justice.*

With the understanding of *karmic* imbalance and reincarnation we can begin to live in justice and mercy. Our spirit knows this truth. If we are just and merciful then there is no need for *karmic* balance or reincarnation. Yet in our addiction to materialism, we have lost contact with justice and mercy. Materialism, as a force, can move us away from our Spirituality into a kind of negative prison. I am not speaking about the need and desire for abundance, but rather the addiction to acquisition. This addiction could be by stealing or spending. Either way there is no peace within. It is not until we can see ourselves as part of the whole that we have the opportunity to be free of this prison.

Some of us believe that it is just to execute those who have been sentenced to death. (The wages of sin is death.) Still, others believe the opposite. Who is right? Let us look at the sub-law of *Cause and Effect*.

The reason we are on the Earth-Plane is to learn who we truly are and then ascend. Part of the lesson we are charged with is to learn to support and love each other as one. If one of us has committed a crime which interferes with another's path, there is an imbalance. If the person is remorseful and committed to helping his/her 'victim' to regain their direction, then what would be the point of retribution? If the lesson is learned, then the goal has been partially reached. *Karmic* indebtedness is balanced.

Our challenge is to understand that compassion and love are based on expanded consciousness. The person in question may have chosen in spirit to be executed in order to reach a balance with the law of karma. Or the person may need to remain on the Earth-Plane in order to learn the lesson. It is not easy for any of us to assess which course of action would benefit both the perpetrator and the 'victim.' We have to remove ourselves from vengeance if we are going to be a positive force for liberation.

Please note that I have put the word victim in quotation

marks. There are no victims. We have created everything that happens to us. Knowing this gives us further direction in our quest for justice. We attract the energies of creativity by positive thoughts or fearful thoughts. This is called the Law of Attraction or the Tool Law, as I call it, which is the power (tool) that can give us direction to be in integrity with each of the Twelve Universal Laws

Exercise #1:

Once again I am asking you to look at your past for an incident that caused you great pain. If this was caused by an individual or an organization, focus on what the motivation was for causing you pain. What compelled them to go in this direction? What benefit did they receive by their actions? In their eyes, do you think they feel that they were justified in hurting you? If you have maintained a relationship with them, how do you think they perceive you now?

Now imagine them taking a different course that avoids causing you pain. What would have happened to them? Would they have suffered? How do you think they would be now? Do you feel you would still be in a positive relationship with them?

Looking at what actually happened and what you have imagined could have happened, do you sense a course of action that you could take to bring a just balance between the two of you? If you can implement this course, you will have brought about justice and a balance with your karma. Please do not forget that we can only lead a horse to water, if they choose not to drink from your well of Spiritual healing, that is their choice. You have done all that you can do and the party that has benefited is you.

Exercise #2:

As you completed the exercises involving visualization, meditation and your breath in the previous Laws, now do the same with the Law of Justice.

1. Before meditation, make a list of all the times that you remember when you felt that you were being just to others. As an example: You may have rescued a person who was being attacked by someone. Or you may have confronted someone who had unjustly hurt another.

2. Then make a second list of the times that you remember that you had been unjust to someone.

3. Next, go into a meditative state and center your attention on your breath. Now as you inhale, visualize bringing the memory of the just act you did into you through your breath. Then exhale the injustice that you in-

flicted on another. Concentrate on bringing this in and casting out the injustice with each breath. Do this as long as you wish.

The longer you visualize justice coming into you and injustice leaving you, the better.

4. Repeat this breath meditation exercise daily using a different justice-injustice combination until you have completed your lists.

THE LAW OF MERCY

Wherein doth sit the dread and fear of kings;
But mercy is above this sceptred sway,
It is enthroned in the hearts of kings,
It is an attribute to God himself,
And earthly power doth then show likest God's
When mercy seasons justice. Therefore, Jew,
Though justice be thy plea, consider this,
That in the course of justice none of us
Should see salvation: we do pray for mercy,
And that same prayer doth teach us all to render
The deeds of mercy.
Shakespeare, The Merchant of Venice

Commiseration, leniency, charity and tolerance are all aspects of the Law of Mercy. The Law of Mercy could not be activated without the Law of Compassion. Mercy demands that we identify with everyone. It is not so much that we forgive but rather understand that allows mercy to flourish.

Mercy must first come from self. The more we understand what is behind the energies of action, the less we will judge in error. So when we let go of judgement and flow with assessment we create opportunity for mercy. Forgiving yourself for your past errors is the first act of complying with the Law of Mercy. It is in this understanding of self that creates understanding and empathy for others and allows us to forgive those who wronged us in the past.

Pain can be our greatest teacher. It seems we humans

only learn from being whacked by a 2 x 4 against the side of our collective heads. (In Australia and New Zealand it would be a 4 x 2.) Yet, in retrospect, we can appreciate what we have learned from pain. It is through our experiences of pain that we can easily identify with other people's pain. So knowing our own path of self discovery, we can empathize and be more merciful with other people's paths.

From this empathetic association, we can begin to employ mercy in our lives. Mercy can only be effective if the person we are sharing mercy with has learned the lesson. Yet, we must challenge ourselves to be merciful unconditionally. We cannot judge whether a person has learned the lesson when we are not privy to all pertinent information of their soul's growth, but this should not dictate mercy. All we can do is be in integrity with the Law and trust that at some point the lesson will be learned. Forgiving is an act of mercy. It is much easier to be merciful if the person receiving our mercy understands truth. The greater challenge for us is to give mercy freely without judgement. We must turn our other spiritual cheek to the supposed offender.

When we mercifully give our understanding, we are giving our most precious gift. We are creating the expression of the Law of One. We are saying that we all stumble and sometimes fall. But if we can forgive and look to what works in the Universe, then we begin to flow with mercy.

Without mercy we cannot heal. Without healing there cannot be growth. Without growth there cannot be illumination. And without illumination we cannot feel and experience a peaceful oneness with all.

Exercise #1:

I would like to explore the novel and/or the movie, 'Silence of the Lambs.' I will assume that you are familiar with this story. There are two key characters in the story. One is a male psychopathic psychiatrist killer and the other is a female FBI agent. The FBI agent needs information that only the imprisoned psychiatrist can give her in her quest to find another psychopathic killer. This sets the stage for an interaction between the doctor and the agent. What we discover is that the psychopathic doctor is extremely clever, smart and destructive. Yet, there lingers in his persona a warped kind of healer which is activated in his interactions and the manipulative games he plays with the agent.

What I am inviting you to do is to examine your assessment and the feelings that you have toward the psychopathic psychiatrist killer. He, of course, is a very frightening character. But what else do you feel for this fictional character? Is there anything that you can learn about yourself from both your reaction to him and your understanding of his illness? If you had unlimited power over such a person, what would your course of action be that you would take in dealing with him and why? Now look at your reaction and see where the Law of Mercy comes into this scenario, if at all. This should give you an idea of where you stand with yourself and this Law.

Exercise #2:

As you completed the exercises involving visualization, meditation and your breath in the previous Laws, now do the same with the 'Law of Mercy.'

1. Before meditation, make a list of all the times that you remember when you felt that you were being merciful to others. As an example: You may have rescued a person who was being attacked by someone. Or you may have confronted someone who had unjustly hurt another.

2. Then make a second list of the times that you remember when you had been unjust to someone.

3. Next, go into a meditative state and center your attention on your breath. Now as you inhale visualize bringing the memory of the just act you did into yourself through your breath. Then exhale the injustice that you inflicted on another. Concentrate on bringing this in and casting out

the injustice with each breath. Do this as long as you wish.

The longer you visualize justice coming into you and in-justice leaving you, the better.

4. Repeat this breath meditation exercise daily using a different justice-injustice combination until you have com-pleted your lists.

THE LAW OF SALVATION

Salvation is deliverance from any energy of thought or action that prevents the individual from being at peace with everyone and everything.

In defining Salvation, we must define:

1. Liberation
2. Freedom
3. Emancipation
4. Rescue
5. Fearlessness

1. *Liberation* can be defined as the state of being after removing the shackles of self-doubt.

2. *Freedom* is using free choice as a tool for teaching and learning. The path to peace can only come in the freedom of choice.

3. *Emancipation* comes when the soul shares consciousness with the material body (brain) and all dimensions of the universe can be felt.

4. *Rescue* comes to the soul when the awareness of one's divinity is constant.

5. Finally, when all *fear* is removed from the total being, one becomes liberated into the *Law of Salvation*. Salvation then, is being in total peace and harmony with everything.

"Buddha was not a Buddhist. Jesus was not a Christian. Be a light unto yourself." What I mean by this saying is that both Siddhartha and Jesus never meant for a religion to be built around them. They wanted each of us to look within as well as outward to find truth and salvation. It was by their example that we have found the best temple, the temple within. Outside of Buddhism, most religions tend to demand subservience rather than teaching enlightenment. Even if religions did teach enlightenment rather than subservience, we would still need to search for the truth within. There are many paths but only one truth. For each of us to find truth we must plot our own course. Since each of us is a universe unto ourselves, we need to be the director of this course. We may find that for a time, a religion helps us to find our course, but in the final revelation, it can only come from within. Trust the wisdom within you to guide you to your own salvation.

Exercise #1:

To do this exercise my suggestion would be for you to record the following and then play it back to yourself as you go into meditation.

Close your eyes and imagine yourself without any fear. You are floating in outer space and looking down on Earth. All of the anxiety, anger and confusion is removed. You have complete clarity of the beauty and love that abounds. You sense the love that Mother Earth has for you and you can feel her need for your love. So as you look at her and feel her love, send her your love. With this exchange you begin to slowly descend and gently land on her surface. Looking around you discover that you have landed on an island in the South Pacific. You seem to be alone until you discover birds, monkeys, lizards and many unusual and varied animals that all seem very happy and friendly. Walking among them, you can sense their love toward you.

Looking to the center of the island, you see many coconut, palm and banana trees. As you walk toward this jungle, you can see orange, lemon, lime, mango, papaya and many different nut trees. In a small opening you see a figure coming toward you. He is tall, straight and very old. With a long white beard and mustache. He is clothed in only a white loin cloth and sandals. His body is very dark, as if he has spent his whole life in the sun. As he draws nearer, you can see him smiling. He greets you and invites you to sit on the grass across from him. At first he says nothing, respectfully waiting for you to be comfortable.

Then he speaks:

"My friend, we have been waiting for you to come to us for many lifetimes. We congratulate you on achieving salvation. Though you have suffered greatly in many of your lives, your addiction to the illusion of fear has prevented you from liberation. Now we can celebrate your evolution away from the imprisonment of fear. You have enriched us all, so we thank you. When one achieves salvation, we all become liberated. Do you understand this my child?" (Pause) "Very well. Now on this Island is everything you need to sustain yourself. We are gifting you this time and place so that you may celebrate. There is one that will join you in your celebration. This is your soul mate who has also achieved salvation. Together we ask only that you enjoy and when you are ready, we will help in your moving toward illumination. Be one with God, my child."

This is the end of your recording. Hopefully you will have a sense of what it feels like to be in the Law of Salvation. In reality, we all have the opportunity to be on this island.

Exercise #2:

The only thing that is immortal with us is our spirit and soul. * *The truth of who we are is not the ego or our temporary body, it is spirit and soul. We are divine. The es-*

86

sence of who we are is hidden from us by our ego (fear). So the challenge in gaining a peace within is to let go of the ego. This exercise, then, is to bring to you a way toward peace.

Envision someone standing in front of you with whom it is difficult to be friendly and/or understanding. This is a person to whom you have trouble relating. The person could be a parent, boss or someone that thinks of you as an enemy. As you watch the drama of this person who strives to dominate, control or anger you, place a huge Buddha, Christ, Mohammed or Krishna behind this person as the serene truth of their being. Understand that their drama is the illusion that they cling to out of anger, fear and confusion and that the huge serene one behind them is the true essence of who they are. Begin to converse, in your mind, with the serene one behind the person. Ask what is preventing this person from recognizing his/her own serenity. Let your imagination give you the answer. Continue to interact with the huge serene one until you feel that you have a better understanding of what motivates this person.

Now, if you can develop a new habit of placing the huge serene one behind each person that you meet, you will begin to shift the consciousness of both yourself and

---

* The molecular structure of the body is also immortal but in a different way. After death it changes into a new form.

the person in front of you. It is our perceptions that create love or fear and our understanding that creates compassion.

Next, be comfortable in placing the serene one behind you as you look in the mirror and recognize it as your True self. Then create a dialog with your serene one to gain clarity of your concept of self. We can only have compassion for others if we let go of the ego and embrace ourselves as equal to all.

The key to understanding the dynamics of this is to acknowledge that we are ALL ONE and that we cannot judge anyone as being inferior, wrong or evil. There is a serene essence to each of us that is our true angelic being.
The potential to become conscious of this comes with letting go of the ego/fear and replacing it with humility and love. Salvation lies in letting go of the ego and control so that we flow with the angelic spirit that we are.

Exercise #3:

As you completed the exercises involving visualization, meditation and your breath in the previous Laws now do the same with the Law of Salvation.

1. Before meditation, take note of the times when you had a new revelation about who you are. Each of us have

had stages of awareness come to us periodically in our lives. See if you can remember yours. As an example: You may have recalled an experience that taught you a profound truth about who you really are.

2. Then make a second list of the times you remember when you felt separate or lonely.

3. Next, go into a meditative state and center your attention on your breath. Now as you inhale visualize bringing the memory of the experience of awareness into yourself through your breath. Then exhale an experience of being separate or lonely. Concentrate on bringing awareness in and casting out the negative illusion with each breath. Do this as long as you wish.

The longer you visualize salvation coming into you and illusion leaving you, the better.

4. Repeat this breath meditation exercise daily using a different combination until you have completed your lists.

THE LAW OF ILLUMINATION

"Illumine, what is low raise and support;
That to the highth of this great argument
I may assert eternaal Providence,
And justify the ways of God to Men."
John Milton, Paradise Lost, bk.i,1.22

Spiritual enlightenment results from the mystical way to perfection when the soul reaches total understanding of the spiritual order in everything. This truth is called the Law of Illumination or the illuminative way.

Flowing within the Law of Illumination demands that there be perfect attunement with all of the other Universal Laws. Illumination is the ending of all struggles. It is reuniting with everything. No longer is there need to reach for the light, for, under the Law of Illumination, you become the Light.* All progress is history. All learning is history. And all knowing is now.

In the creative energies you become a representation of perfection. You become one with all. Being one with all, you are unlimited.

---

* In "Talks With Christ," channeled by Elwood Babbitt, Lochia talks about light. "I would not call it light, but a ray of Life Force designed to increase the wisdom of man's spirit."

In the *Law of Illumination*, the answers to the meaning of all things are found. Illumination is the law of perfect truth. Illumination is not something to be achieved but a state that is. Only in becoming aware of this law is the law activated. Only by being constantly in integrity with the other universal laws can there be illumination.

The *Law of Illumination* is enlightenment, which is the fullness of knowing and the companion of wisdom.

In Japanese Zen Buddhism, enlightenment can be obtained through two paths of experiencing: *Satori* and/or *Kensho*. These are experiential degrees of a momentary awareness. The more these are experienced, the closer the individual is to becoming Buddha. Yet, I believe that anyone can experience *Satori* and/or *Kensho* and thus Buddhahood through the loving discipline of these 12 laws. It is my contention that if you become conscious of each of these Laws in a loving habitual daily relationship, the attainment of Illumination is most probable.

Exercise #1:

This exercise can only be effective if you are in a state of peace. If during the exercise you become depressed, unhappy or agitated, please stop. Play some music, have a cup of coffee or tea and relax back into a peaceful state. Then you can continue.

Ask yourself: When was I last unhappy? What were the circumstances in the situation? Who did I believe was involved with my unhappiness?

Take time to remember why you were unhappy. As you look at your unhappiness ask yourself: Did I play any part in creating my own unhappiness? If so, what was it that I did that caused this condition?

Don't get caught in the trap of thinking that your unhappiness was caused by something or by what someone else did or said to you. As the captain of your own ship you are the only one in charge of steering your course in life's waters. No one can control you or your feelings unless you allow it. So if someone seemed to hurt you, you had a preconditioned reaction that you allowed yourself to be hurt. The question is, what was the historic cause of your preconditioned reaction? If you can get to this cause then you could have a better understanding of why you reacted the way you did. With this understanding you can now release its hold on you. So the next time a similar situation occurs it won't effect you as it had.

If someone called you an S.O.B. and you got mad and wanted to retaliate, that would be one reaction. If, on the other hand, you were called a S.O.B. and you realized that the person was laboring under his/her own past patterns of hate behavior, then your reaction may be one of pity.

It is in looking into your past experiences of pain that

you can better understand what has been controlling your unhappy reactions to life's 'negative' conditions. The more you explore your history of pain, in this fashion, the greater your sense of liberation and joy can be.

Exercise #2:

As you completed the exercise for Salvation, I invite you to tape record the following and then play it back to yourself as you go into meditation.

Since you have activated the illuminative way, you'll discover that your physical body is no longer a restriction. You can freely move about the universe unencumbered by anything. This new found freedom excites you as you move into new areas of exploration. (Pause)

As you look around the vast array of stars and galaxies, you are attracted to a beautiful multicolored round cylinder that is elongated. It appears to be a cloud of dust because you can see stars through the other side of it. You decide to investigate, so you move yourself forward. As you approach this colorful cloud you realize that it is remnant debris left over from a supernova. The shape intrigues you as you focus on it. As you look at it, you are moved back in time and see this massive star expanding and turning red just before the explosion. Witnessing this phenomenon gives you a complete understanding of the creative shift of energies. Feeling this power, you sense that you could create something new and wonderful from this remnant debris. Understanding this creative force within you and using your imagination, you decide to create a new solar system. Even though you acknowledge that this would be the first time you have thought of doing something like this, let alone knowing that you can, you are excited to do it anyway. (Slight pause)

Near by is a cluster of dark matter along with dark energy which you can use to create. So you draw this to the cloud and surround it with the dark matter and dark energy. Now you begin to compress the cloud with the dark matter and energy. As you do this, you can see a change taking place in the core of the cloud cylinder. The debris is being transformed into a nuclear force. (Pause)

As this compaction continues, you understand that you can also create satellite bodies around the core. Understanding the Laws of Order, Balance and Harmony you choose varying sizes and compositions to compliment the core. As you work, you also decide to reduce the size of the original massive star and use the rest of the matter to create more satellites. (Pause)

In the back of your mind, you acknowledge that you have a desire to create new life forms on some of the satellite planets. So as the solar system nears completion, you begin to focus on how you would want these life forms to look. You are tempted to copy what you are familiar with from your experiences on Earth. Yet, you decide to be more creative and try something new and different. You are not interested in striving for a utopian type of life but rather, you want to maintain your integrity with the creative law of Growth. So in this regard you will copy the evolution of consciousness that you experienced on Earth and incorporate this into all of your life forms. Now as you are focused on this creation, allow your imagination to take you wherever you want to go, knowing that there is no limitation except the restraints you wish to impose upon yourself. Take all the time you want in order to feel complete with this phase of the exercise.

After coming out of your meditation please review what you have created in your meditative state. Does any of this give you an idea of your own awareness toward Illumination? Can you now better understand the logic and reasoning of the ongoing expansion of all life toward a higher consciousness? Through this exercise do you not feel God's love and expectation for your liberation into enlightenment? I hope so, because I believe this is what life is all about.

Exercise #3:

Seat yourself before a mirror. Look at your face first and smile, then focus on your third eye, which is the area above and between your eyes. Concentrate your whole being on this area. Give yourself plenty of time to be completely absorbed into your psyche. Concentrate on your magnificence by saying over and over to yourself: "I am light, I am perfect, I am Love." As you continue to say this mantra, open your heart to God's love as you also send your love to God. Stay with this until you feel a joy of oneness.

QUESTIONNAIRE
(This pertains to all Twelve Laws)

These questions are designed to help clarity some of the major issues that confront humanity at this time. If each of us can answer these questions based on what we have learned about the Laws, we will gain an insight that we would't have gained otherwise. This is an exercise that will both challenge and empower you at the same time. Going past your initial reaction to the question is the first step. As best you can, divorce yourself from any emotional attachment that you may have with these questions. Endeavor to view the question as a quest to understand how the universal Laws of Vishnu are applicable.

My invitation is for you to come back to these questions in one or two years to see if your answers are different. If they are, your assessment may have been influenced by new experiences of wisdom or a shift in your consciousness.

Use a loose leaf note book and write down each question and answer on separate pages.

1. What Law(s) would you be against or with if you gamble? Why?

2. Have you ever been sold something for more than it was worth? Which Law(s) do you believe were violated either by the seller or you as the purchaser because of this act, if any?

3. When you file income tax, are you out of integrity with any of the Laws? Is the I R S out of integrity with any of the Laws?

4. Aside from the Law of Truth, which other Laws do you see yourself in violation of when you lie?

5. What Universal Laws, if any, do insurance companies violate? Explain and elaborate.

6. If creating nuclear energy violates any of the *Universal Laws*, which ones and why? If nuclear energy does not violate the Laws, please explain.

7. If a person is addicted to acquiring material wealth, which of the Laws are being violated? What Laws are being violated if the addiction is to poverty? Explain both.

8. Does it go against any of Vishnu's Laws to domesticate animals? Why? If domestication is not in violation of the Laws, explain.

9. Is being a herbivorous person in greater alignment with the Laws than being a carnivorous person? If so, why?

10. Does the taking of recreational drugs or alcohol go against any of the Laws? Elaborate please.

11. If a doctor prescribes a drug that could have damaging side effects, would you be in violation of any of the Laws if you took it?

12. If you are a member of a religion, is this religion in compliance with the Laws of Vishnu? What are your observations of the religions of the world in regard to the Laws of Vishnu?

13. What Laws are violated by a dictator? What Laws would the population under the dictator be violating?

14. Are any of the Laws of God being violated by abortion? Please answer in detail so that you give credence to your position.

15. Are any of the Laws being violated by the act of suicide? Again answer in detail so that you give credence to your position.

16. If a friend of yours was wounded and in enormous pain, and there was no way of saving his or her life would you kill your friend to relieve the suffering? What Laws would you be with or against, because of this action?

17. What Laws would or would not be violated by having quotas on minorities in schools or in the work place?

10. Is driving a car going against any of the Laws?

19. When we are in the energies of greed, which of the Laws are we violating?

20. When we are in the energies of hate, which of the Laws are we violating?

21. Is the medical community out of integrity with any of the Laws?

22. Is our judicial system in compliance with the Laws or not?

23. Is the condition of pride (ego) in compliance with the Laws? Please elaborate.

CONCLUSION

I believe that each of us, in our own way, is reaching for Illumination. Whether we are aware of this is not relevant. It is a natural drive toward the answer to the question "Why," that I mentioned at the beginning of this book. These 12 Laws have come to us from Spirit (Vishnu) or if you wish God and as such, their observed energies are our guides toward Nirvana or enlightenment If we allow ourselves to move from fear to love.

This concludes my presentation of these Laws. It has been a collaboration with Spirit and an extraordinary journey for me. I have been honored to have had this experience. If you wish to share your thoughts, reactions and experiences from this, I would be most grateful. You can reach me at either:

www.Santireadings.com   or

sasasanti12@gmail.com

Please put "12 Laws" in the subject line.

May you have a loving and compassionate journey toward illumination.

SOURCES

I   "The God Within, A Testament of Vishnu"

II "Talks With Christ and His Teachers"

III "Voices of Spirit"
    by Elwood Babbitt and Charles Hapgood
    Fine Line Books, PO Box 281, Turners Falls,
    MA 01376
    Amazon.com

IV "The Circulating Files" of Universal Laws
    The A.R.E. 67th St. and Atlantic Ave.
    PO Box 595, Virginia Beach, VA
    23451-0595.
    Phone 1-804-428-3588

V   "Delta Spectrum Research,
    Pond Science Institute"
    921 Santa Fe Avenue, La Junta, CO 81050
    dalesvp@centurytel.net, or www.svpvril.com

VI "The Essential Unity of All Religions"
    by Bhagavan Das

SOURCES (Continue)

VII "The Sufis"
     by Idries Shah

VIII "The Trilogy of The Law of Attraction"
     1. "The Law of Attraction"
     2. "Money, and the Law of Attraction"
     3. "The Vortex"
     by Esther and Jerry Hicks
     Hay House, Inc.